Kinetic Kopy

This book and it's content under copyright Phantom Script Publishing © 2015.

Phantom Script Publishing
2602 Turner Street
Muskogee, OK 74403

phantomscriptg@live.com

ISBN-13:
978-1516947591

ISBN-10:
1516947592

Copyright © Imagery Magic Solutions

Kinetic Kopy

"Probably one of the most important things you need to know in marketing."

LEGAL NOTICE

The author and publisher have strived to be as accurate and complete as possible in the creation of this report, notwithstanding the fact that they do not warrant or represent at any time that the contents within are completely accurate at the time which you are reading due to the rapidly changing nature of the Internet and marketing in general.

While all attempts have been made to verify information provided in this publication, the author or the publisher assumes no responsibility for errors, omissions, or contrary interpretation of the subject matter herein. Any perceived slights of specific persons, peoples, or organizations are coincidental and totally unintentional.

In practical advice books, like anything else in life, there are no guarantees of income made. Readers are cautioned to rely on their own judgment about their individual circumstances.

This book is not intended for use as a source of legal, business, accounting or financial advice. All readers are advised to seek the services of competent professionals.

Copyright © Imagery Magic Solutions

Now, That being said, I hope that the information in this book helps you to get a better understanding of copywriting.

All rights reserved.
For more information, contact Phantom Script Publishing at phantomscript@live.com.

Copyright © Imagery Magic Solutions

Table of Contents

	Introduction	5
	Headers That Sell	7
	From Header to Headline	10
	Sub Headlines, Coaxing Curiosity	14
	Opening your Letter	16
	Features and Benefits	21
	Bonuses	22
	Guarantee	23
	Walk Your Customer through Order Process	25
	Getting Effective Testimonials	27
	More Tips	28
	Resources & Bonuses	30

Kinetic Kopy

The application of effective copywriting is an ongoing process that I've personally been working on perfecting from day one when I first became aware that good copy could make you a living while great copy could make you a fortune.

You see, great copywriting skills are one of the single most important skills you can ever learn in marketing. You either learn to write it, or pay someone else to write it for you. Personally... I was one who would rather learn it myself and keep that kind of money in my own pocket as well as maybe earn some by writing for others.

Even if you decide to pay someone else to do your copy for you, it is always a good idea to grasp basic fundamentals of copy writing so that you don't find yourself paying large sums of money for copy that doesn't convert.

It doesn't matter how fantastic your products or services are... if your sales copy stinks then you will find out the hard when you see your time and money go down the drain.

However, on the other hand, you can have a very poor product, but if your sales copy screams "You can't live without this"... Then it can sell big.

I'm sure you've experienced this before... You find yourself so engrossed in a sales page that you have to re-read it, show someone else or even pull out your credit card. This is the experience that you are aiming toward when you write your own copy.

Copyright © Imagery Magic Solutions

Kinetic Kopy

In fact, this doesn't just apply to sales pages, it applies to web pages, social media sites, hard copy, everything... Have you ever had an ad that comes on TV... and you find yourself intensely paying attention to what they are selling? You feel compelled to watch every part of it... You know you're being "sold to" but you just can't resist. You've got to watch it until the end. There are actually people who watch the super bowl every year just for the commercials.

You are about to learn some of the secrets that professional copywriters know and use to get higher conversions on all of their sales copy. Whether it is email marketing, social media or direct marketing, this formula will give you higher conversions on your sales copy.

Enjoy and I wish you the best on your future copy projects.

Copyright © Imagery Magic Solutions

Headers That Sell

Effective headers catch the viewer's attention initially from a peripheral view. They are (or should be) the primary focus of the ad piece. Notice I said primary and not main… A properly placed header can make your headline pop.

Let me explain…

First you want to come up with something that catches visual attention. If the header blends too much with the rest of the copy then the entire copy will get lost as a visual block of text as opposed to "Hey, Look At Me!"

Second, you don't always have to come up with a snappy one-liner. In fact, that actually turns some readers off. Just make sure that the header says something that catches the reader's attention.

A word of warning; the header must lead into the copy and can't just be an attention getter. You want it to enhance and not take away the focus from what you are selling.

Now we need to discuss aesthetics. How does it look? Colors work great in creating urgency, expressing warmth, and visually attracting (or repelling) your audience. This is true online and in printed hardcopy. Online, a bright green font on a bright blue background can give you a headache, while dark blue text on a light blue background is actually soothing to the eyes.

If you are using a blue background then a red colored header is going to look inappropriate. Yes… it will stand out, but it will also give the viewer eye-stain. This same effect happens on hardcopy as well, especially if you are using a thin or small font.

Now that I have said all of this, I now say that headers aren't always necessary. As in any and all marketing, know your audience, know how you want to present it and know what sales best.

Another thing that is becoming more utilized online, it the use of background images as opposed to colors.

See how the image above kind of draws you in without saying a word?

Another final thought on headers is one that I alluded to earlier, but bares more mention and that is that you want your headers to play into your body, but it also needs to play into your call-to-action. If an ad piece is too long, many people will skim over it first to see if there is anything of interest, so if your header at the top and your call to action match up, then that tells them that there is continuity in the piece and if the header and the call to action both spark interest, they are more likely to read through the piece and not just look over it.

Note: as of the writing of this report, studies show that bright orange is the color that gets the most attention when it comes to headers. Orange background with dark blue or black text, for example; the warm color frames dark text very well. Placed next to colors such as lime green, it can look amazing and "eye-catching".

From Header to Headline

This has been said to be the most crucial part of your sales copy. If the header is the primary focus, then this is your secondary (or main) focus and it really goes without saying. Even if you forgo the header to save on cost, size, etc.; the headline is definitely important to catching attention. Where as the header is visual, the headline is both visual and audible.

What I mean by this is that it is visual because it catches the attention with its size, color, etc., but the headline, itself will catch and/or keep attention with what it says. Catchy slogans, cute titles, erythematic word patterns, etc. are audible in the sense that, as the reader sees, them, they are reading it and hearing themselves read it in their head. If it has flow, remember-ability (if that's really a word) and "catchiness" then it will not only catch attention, but it will lead the reader to see what else is in the text and will lead them into the ad.

How often have you passed over an ad because it didn't catch your attention?

Example would be, while reading in a magazine, you skim over the text:

"Understand Self-Motivation"

Not as catchy because it is flat and impersonal. However, by tweaking it just a little to have more pizzazz and maybe a little more personal to the reader:

"Why We Do What We Do, Understanding Self-Motivation"

We have now personalized it and made it catchier to the eye.
This is the best time to "create" curiosity. So now let's see what it looks like when you add it to a header.

See how the perspective in the image visually opens up to the text, leading your eyes right to it? The image gives a feel of motion, a.k.a. movement that is sometimes visually associated with motivation?

I've also found by using personalizing pronouns such as "YOU" or "WE" in headline seems to convert better. Speak to your visitor right from the get go, The sooner you make them feel the product is for them specifically, the more likely they are to purchase, sign up or do whatever your call-to-action may be.

Its human nature for us to all want to hear about ourselves, talk about ourselves, we all want to know what "you" can do for "me" and not what "I" can do for you.

It has been said that the most loved words a person can hear is the sound of his or her own name. So you want to personalize your header as well as the speech within the rest of the ad.

In fact… this can be your one and only calling card to pitch at them, so always look at your copy from the "what's in it for me" perspective of your readers straight away and get more views.

Tell them in the headline what they will get out of reading your copy.

Like in our example with the self-motivation, I personalized it without indicating that "you" need to understand why YOU do what YOU do.

Notice how I used the word "we". Sometimes, when dealing with more sensitive issues, you may want to use words such as "we" and "us" so that the topic doesn't sound accusing.

There can be a major shift in acceptance between "what YOU need to know" and "what WE need to know" if the topic is touchy.

By using words such as "we" then you are associating yourself with the situation and anyone reading it dealing with that situation gets a sense that you aren't selling to them, but more so that you are, or have been, where they are and understand what they are going through.

A mistake that I sometimes see is someone using a full paragraph as his or her headline. This isn't necessary, and in most cases, will cause the reader to not delve deeper into the ad because they get the feeling that the headline basically gave them all of the info they needed about that ad.

The headline should give a basic eye-catcher to the copy and if you need to, you can use a small paragraph as a sub-headline to help lead readers into the rest of the copy.

Another important factor when you create your headline is the color, font style and font size.

This should stand out more than any other part of your sales page. I usually make this the largest size possible without it looking gaudy.

The font needs to be readable and bold. My favorite is "Verdana"… Here is an example:

"Why We Do What We Do"
Understanding Self-Motivation

The headline is bold, primary and the color stands out and is eye-catching, while the sub-headline is a part of the headline, but is obviously its own line. It adds to the headline without taking away from the emphasis of the main headline. At the same time, it delves a little more into what the content is about.

So many times I have seen some good copy out there, but most people don't see it because they can't get past the headline. The headline and sub-headline are dull, boring and basically detract from the copy.

Guess what though, It's an easy fix!

If you're not pulling good conversions… consider your headline first… get others opinions…There are a lot of great resources for creating good headlines. Don't be afraid to run it up the flagpole and see who solutes.

Sub Headlines
Coaxing Curiosity

This is almost as important as your headline itself. If your sub headline isn't creating a link between your headline and your body content you can lose the reader just as fast as having a bad headline or no headline at all.

Keep creating more curiosity to what you are offering without telling them a complete overview of what is in the content.

Take for example the headline that we already have:

"Why We Do What We Do"
Understanding Self-Motivation

In this sub headline I have answered somewhat, what the topic is about, but I haven't given a complete syllabus so it leads to more curiosity.

You will notice in the example… I've made the sub headline still very large, but yet smaller than the main headline. It is also a different color. I will usually have the sub headline the same color as the body content to help with visual transition.

I find this to be important because you don't want your sub headline to steal the attention of your main headline nor do you want it to completely blend in to the main content. You simply want to hold and maintain the interest of your readers.

Opening Your Letter

I wanted to put this in here because I want to stress that anything you do in a sales piece can also translate into email marketing. Some believe that email marketing is dead because of the many different ways that your email can be "diverted" from being read and thus lead people away from using it to market.

I believe that there is no marketing strategy that completely dies; it just takes on new attributes. The same holds true for email marketing and everything in this report can be effectively used to spice up your emails.

Hopefully, the following visual guides can help you get more emails open.

Email Headline...Think in these terms when you are creating a subject for your subject line. Obviously, you can't change font size, color, etc., but you can put something there that catches attention and doesn't sound like spam.

Then there is the content of the message. With many of the new filters on emails today, you can have an absolutely beautiful html driven email that rivals your website, but what many of your readers will see, it text with all graphics removed.

Try to make your email stand alone without all of the bells and whistles. In rich text format, you can still apply bold, italic, color, highlights, font selection and size.

Create sub headlines in your body text to break up paragraphs.

Work in an option to click a hyperlink to view the email in it's original state. The link can take them to an html document that you can have all of the bells and whistles in, a sales page or even a blog or newsletter.

After a sub headline to get their attention, you want to actually address the reader personally… Hey, [someone] and then a greeting.

Notice that I didn't use "dear". This is because emails using this opening actually detract more than they inspire due to so many solicitations starting with this very word. It has become impersonal and dry. Remember to greet your reader the way you would greet them if they were standing in front of you.

Don't just jump into the sale. Honestly greet them. This is where you go from getting their attention to creating a connection.

Now that a connection is established, you can lead into the sales letter with a build up. From this point on, it is pretty much the same copy that you would have in any other sales material.

Usually a lead in question is a good way to get the transition started.

Kinetic Kopy

Subject: [reader's name here], Why do we do the things we do?

Have you ever asked yourself why some people are great at self-motivation while some of us need a constant kick in the pants?

Hey [someone],

I can't tell you how many times I have pondered this same question. I hope that this email catches you having a great day...

I am not going to write an entire email, because your email will be different depending on what your content is about, therefore it will change. Remember the secret to a good email is to make it feel personal and personal from me won't always sound personal from you, you are the one that knows your audience. It has to capture how you would speak naturally.

An overview example would be at this point, to mention the problem, then associate yourself with having had the same problem, issue, background, etc. in order to build trust and camaraderie with the reader.

This should be about a one to two paragraph build-up.

The next thing you want to do is go into the things that you tried, discovered, learned, etc. that brought you to the answer that you have found.

Copyright © Imagery Magic Solutions

Next, give them the details of the answer a.k.a the solution that you are marketing, but give it in an offer to sign up for more content, free training, free downloads, etc. Don't solicit what you are trying to sell in the first email. You want to "capture" their email address and get permission to solicit to them with future emails; otherwise you are spamming which isn't cool.

Giving free content also helps build trust as well as places you in their minds as an authority in that subject.

Once you have built credibility through a short series of emails with free content. This is where you can begin your direct marketing campaign…so to speak.

Give them the solutions that you have been building up to.

At this point, there are some that are going to want to buy from you now and you should give them an opportunity. Add a call-to-action then go back into the benefits of what you are trying to market. The longer your piece, the more you want to break it up with multiple call-to-action breaks.

Now is the time to back up your credibility with some testimonials… I have found three is a good number to use. Too many and it will bore the reader, only one and it makes them suspicious.

Don't just take it from me… listen to what others have to say when they tried this…

[Testimonial goes here]

[Testimonial goes here]

[Testimonial goes here]

Try to ensure you add a name and where they live. We will discuss more about testimonials later.

Now if you don't want to do rich text and want to take a risk that your html email will not be seen, then I would suggest on using photos and headers to create breaks and transitions.

Photos bring greater credibility… it paints a picture in the mind of the reader.

They do this exact same thing in the "infomercials". In fact… something I've noticed from these types of commercials is most of their advertisement IS testimonials.

ANY documentation of proof you have… ADD it! It will only add to your credibility and ensure your reader your not just pulling their leg.

This may have been an odd place to add this small excerpt about email marketing, but I just wanted to make sure that I made you aware of how these copy techniques could be used.

Features/Benefits

There has always been the great debate between some top copywriters screaming "State benefits not features" and others that say the complete opposite…

Well my simple solution was just state both!

This is where you really need to get creative and stick the meat in with the potatoes.

For example:

- *Using this one particular everyday household product will take that stench out and have your lawn smelling like roses instantly!*

- *Once you use this little doozy NO dog or stray cat will even dare mark your yard as their territory again.*

You know the old saying… Curiosity killed the cat? Well using bullet points like this will drive your reader crazy with curiosity he probably won't even think twice about ordering! He WILL want to know!

Oddly enough… I've even read sales pages where I'm not particularly interested in what they're selling, but the bullet points have created so much curiosity I felt compelled to want to know the "great" hidden secret they had ready for me to find out about at the end of the page.

After stating all of features the product or service gives… I would then immediately progress into stating all of the benefits that the product has…

Example:

- Imagine never having to feel the embarrassment ever again of inviting friends and family over

- Walking out on your front lawn to the smell of freshly mowed lawn and not cat urine

- Imagine going out to pick up the morning paper and not stepping in a *present* left by the neighbor's dog

Bonuses

And if all that wasn't enough to sweeten the pot… You slam on the bonuses.

Now, a fatal error I had made in the earlier days is I didn't add a value to my bonuses, at least until a mentor of mine called me on it. I was asked… "Don't you value your bonuses? Because if you don't value them then why should your customers?"

It was a reality shot between the eyes… but a good one nonetheless! You see, if you give your readers a free report that has no stated value, you might as well take the text from the report and insert it into an email as free content.

However, if you offer a free report, download, etc. that has a value attached to it, then your reader feels that they are getting a good deal.

You now see many sales copy pieces now that give added bonuses that will actually have an estimated price of what the bonus would normally cost as well as bullet points of some features/benefits of each added bonus.

Next Step…

Guarantee

This has always been one of the great debates in marketing… most say you "have" to give your pitch a guarantee. In today's society of spammers and online con artists, creating trust with your readers is vital and many will not buy now unless there is a guarantee. I can personally validate that a guarantee does pull more sales.

The fear is that there will be a lot of refund requests. Actually, this is not the case. I have tested different methods of writing a guarantee to "lessen" the amount of refund requests that come through, but even this isn't necessary. I mean, if you make a percentage of sales with no guarantee with no returns, then a guarantee that doubles your sales allows for you to do a few refunds and still make more profit than you would have.

Now, all of this is being said under the idea that your product or service is good. Lipstick on a pig is just a prettier pig. That being said there are certain ways that you can write your guarantee to lessen the amount of refund requests.

Maximum possible amount of sales then tell them in your guarantee…

Example:

100% 30 Day No Questions Asked – NO if's, and's or but's Guarantee
If you're not completely happy with this product even if you so much as spot a cat hair within 5-yards of your front porch then I want you to email me right away for a prompt and courteous full refund of your money!

After this, I like to add the next paragraphs to expand on how much of a good deal they're getting.

In one paragraph, I compare my price to what they might pay for a similar product elsewhere and this adds value to the product which makes them less likely to return it.

Another great way to increase perceived value is by initially making the price point higher.

Example:

This normally sells for $1,000 but if you order today you get this plus the added bonuses for only $497.

This will usually give the reader a sigh of relief and excited that he is getting it at this bargain price in which many take on an almost slight sense of guilt at the thought of asking for a refund because they bought it for a fraction of it's value.

Walk Your Customer through the Steps of Ordering

The first words I begin with in this process are:

Place Your Risk-Free Order Now using our Secure Server Provided

Straight off the bat I'm asking them to place their order at the same time soothing their doubts about ordering online by letting them know about the secure server used to process the payment.

This is also a good time to mention "how" they will receive the goods they're ordering. i.e. Will it be emailed? Is it downloadable? If it's a physical product such as a book, how will it be shipped and how long will it take to arrive?

Sign your letter off!

Sincerely,
<Your name here>

Set up your order button. You will want this to be outstanding. Not something they will skim past un-noticed. Placing an **order here** can easily be over-looked.

Remember that you want your order button to stand out from the rest of the text such as the example given earlier.

Copyright © Imagery Magic Solutions

Then hit them with a strong P.S.

This is where you create the urgency and need to buy right now

Example:

P.S. This offer is for a time limited only, we have a limited supply in stock.

Then you want to add a P.P.S when possible to end with an emotional reminder of what the product can do for them. People shop with intellect, but buy on emotion.

Example:

P.P.S. A great smelling lawn is just minutes away, don't delay

Etc.. etc..

Getting effective testimonials

Though testimonials are not the easiest to get, at least good ones that go beyond the dull one-liners, it is possible to get some great ones that can be used in your marketing.

Your customer doesn't realize how much of an impact a testimonial can have on your business and will rarely give one without being asked. To bad this isn't the case for negative feedback.

It is sometimes difficult to solicit testimonials, so here's an idea you can utilize to increase the quantity and quality of your testimonials…

Send out an "unadvertised" bonus a few days after their purchase… Completely free of charge! On the page add a feedback form with a few questions.

Some example questions might be:

Could you tell us your story as to what's brought about X problem?
What results have you received from using our product?
Would you recommend this product to others? If so, who do you think it would be most suited to?
Do you believe you got value for your money?

Then simply ask permission to correlate this into a testimonial you can use on your web page, sales material, email marketing campaign, etc.

More Tips

Tables – Use one! How horrible is it when you go to a website and you've got to read from one side of the page to the other without a neat and small table? Unpleasant isn't it?

Backgrounds – They say that blue backgrounds (more specifically, Robins egg blue, **#00CCCC**) are the tried and tested and pull the greater response. I also agree with going with a theme as long as you keep it consistent and not too busy.

For example – if you're selling something about love, then set the mood with a red or soft pink background; if you're selling golf tips then an emerald green background would be a suitable theme.

Your main text should be on a white background with black text. Don't use fancy and/or hard to read font styles. You want the page to be as "readable" as possible.

Add visuals to your products. If it's a digital product you can still bring it to life by creating a digital 3D look and appearance.

Kinetic Kopy

If you can't accomplish this, I always suggest going to http://www.fiverr.com/ to find quality talent that will create a create looking digital cover for $5.

==Hi-lighting== – This is effective, provided that you use it sparingly… It will lose its effect if over used. Make sure you only use this to hi-light dramatic important parts in your copy. <u>The same holds true for underlining</u>.

I have covered quite a few of the basics here that I hope you have found informative and useful. Here is to your success. Don't just market; be persuasive.

Resources & Bonuses

I want to first leave you with some resources that have helped me get to where I am in the field of effective copywriting.

The first resource that I want to give you is a mentor of mine that I have followed for years and would have never had the inspiration or the drive to follow my dream if not for this guy.

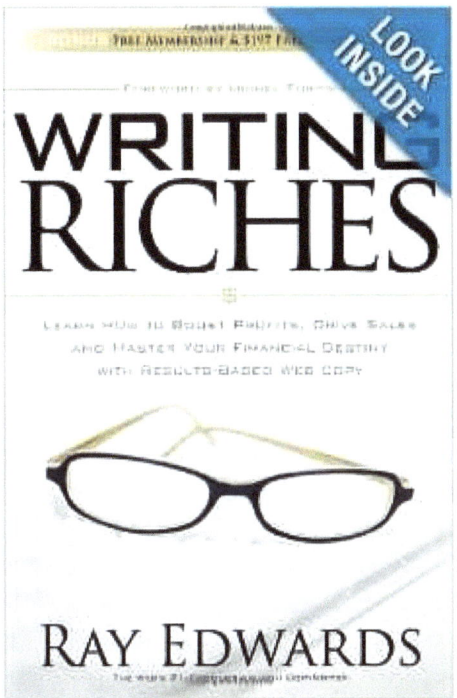

Ray Edwards is a living legend in the field of effective copy and if you are looking to move to the next level fast, then I recommend getting the book that you see above. It is a best seller for a reason; this guy knows his stuff.

If you are satisfied with what you have learned from this book and want to move on to more detailed marketing ideas that go beyond copywriting then I recommend checking out the following:

Dan Kennedy is another legend when it comes to marketing. His ability to think outside of the box and put new shine to old processes is amazing. If you are looking for ideas and training on direct marketing, then this book is for you.

If you are looking for sales help, then I highly recommend the following book by Zig Ziglar. He recently passed away in 2012 after a long career in sales and motivation.

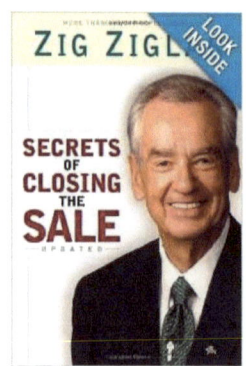

Now for a bonus…

The following is an excerpt from a piece I worked on about branding, which goes hand in hand with effective marketing and copy.

As a business owner for over 5 years now, I have found that branding is very important for any business that is looking to expand and move forward in today's economy. A company's brand is like the glue that differentiates it from all of it's competitors. In today's world of economic turbulence and uncertainty, it's vital for many to most businesses, no matter what your field, to have a remembered presence in order to remain competitive. Effective branding can create a visual imprint in the minds of your clients. Simply put, whether online or off line, branding helps you get and stay remembered.

Brand Your Way To Success
Simple Branding Techniques That Work

While branding can offer vast opportunities for your business, whether you are the CEO of a top 500 company or a blogger using affiliate marketing to add additional revenue to your account, in order for it to be great and serve you well, we need to first draw in and engage our clients. This isn't as easy as it sounds, but if done correctly, it can bring you in a bounty of new and interested clients as well as keeping the old ones engaged and eager to continue coming back. Unfortunately, branding isn't as simple as putting your company logo and motto on a business card or (now days) creating a social media page. The branding strategy that you use must make your brand not only noticeable, but relevant in your market place so that a client sees you as a trusted authority and thinks of you first. If I say, "Just Do It" we all know what company that I am talking about. The same holds true if you see a webding style image of an apple with a bite taken out of the top.

Branding Basics
New Perspective

Branding, especially when you are working with online branding, has many tools at our disposal that we can utilize to produce a visual presence for our business that makes our companies pop when it comes to making a visual impression, and many of them are inexpensive to free. Web graphics and animation, great web copy, and your overall website design, a killer logo and tagline are just a few of the significant factors that will bring your brand alive. This magnetic appeal that helps your viewers easily and quickly think of you first when they need what you provide is the number one most fundamental key to turning viewers into paying customers. The branding that you use should include great design and factor in a visual uniqueness that visually captivates interest when producing your total impression.

The Branding Reflection: Your Visual Presence
A strong, easy to recognize image can make the difference between someone who buys from you or goes on to your competition. For example, a client online, can easily go from your site to your competitor's by simply double clicking their mouse. First impressions are everything and a lot hinges on the impression they get from your web site, your newspaper ads, or any other advertising media that you use. Branding, or so I have found, conveys a unique message about who you and your business is to your target market.

There many requirements for a successful branding campaign. If you are totally out of your element here, you could try to hire a branding agent to help give you some ideas, but before you do, continue reading. My goal is to give you some pointers and hopefully encourage you in creating your brand without spending hundreds, if not thousands on branding.

Baby Steps
Taking it slow so you don't fall short
I discussed the importance of having a great, easy to recognize logo, but branding is much more than simply having your logo or slogan and it's more than simply using a unique color scheme on all of your documents. Here are some initial baby steps to take that need to happen in order to begin your successful brand creation.

First steps
Where To Start

Analyze Your Competition

Probably the number one key, as I have come to use many times over in my own business as well as helping others, is to produce a successful brand by differentiating yourself from your competition. You will have to know how buyers see your competitors and then, equally as important, know how they see you in comparison to your competition.

You must recognize how your competitors set themselves apart from their competition. In addition, you should also make yourself aware of all of the areas in which they excel as well as fall short in. Your business may benefit more from knowing where your competitors drop the ball than from where they are killing it, and learn how to use their shortcoming to distinguish your company from the rest of the pack.

Show...Know your muscles: Identify your strengths

Now, after you recognize where the competitors are dropping the ball when it comes to how the client sees them, you are able to start cross-comparing their weaknesses with your strengths, because their weak areas need to be part of your company's strengths in order to catch the eye of the clients they are turning away because of the weaknesses. You can perform a target market analysis (formal or impromptu), learn from it, and utilize it in every way that you can to your advantage. This is a valuable tool when first creating your name in the market place.

Once you've recognized AND LISTED your strengths, and made note of which ones are most significant to your clients, you should be able to think about ways to successfully market these assets and incorporate them in your branding campaign. For example, when I started my engraving company, it was really difficult to find engravers that would personalize individual gifts purchased elsewhere. Part of my slogan and our mission statement was "We make your memories more personal." I also incorporated quite a few pictures of original, one of a kind engravings on the website to catch attention. Through this we, not only gained more clients, but actually had some of our "competitors" sending jobs our way.

Hark! Who goes there? Know YOUR client

Learn everything you can about your target market. Know their buying habits. How often do they purchase? Do they have a habit of only purchasing during special promotions? How detailed are they when purchasing? what I mean by this is, do they stick to specific name brands, are their only certain sites they visit online?

These are questions you really need to ask to better market to those that you serve. In addition to that, know your buyer's lifestyles, needs, mentalities, and attitudes. Knowing and working with things such as personality traits and shopping habits are key to your marketing success with these potential clients.

Think da brand, know da brand, BE da brand

Make certain your company truly reflects what your brand identifies. As another example, if one of the traits your brand attaches to your company is professionalism, then show professionalism in every aspect of your business. If your website hasn't been updated in years and still references a sale or event that happened years ago, this isn't professional. If you have a brick and mortar place of business and it is disorganized with employees looking disheveled, this also does not reflect professionalism.

Be the Guru
Become the expert that your client needs
Demonstrating yourself as an authority in your field will help you acquire both recognition and respect from your peers, your competition and, most importantly, your clients. Like I mentioned earlier, I actually had competitors sending me clients.

When those around you see you as the expert, you become the expert, i.e. you become the first one they think of when they need the product or service that you provide.

This is where good visual and auditory branding come in to play.

Making the Grade
Some things to think about when creating

Now you are probably saying "FINALLY!" I know, the preceding was kind of long winded, but it was important to lay some groundwork out before jumping into the actual physics of branding. You can have the best logo in the world, but if it doesn't represent what you do, then it is a lost cause and could actually end up repelling potential customers.

The Logo

A big mistake many businesses get into when they first come up with a logo is to try to make this ornate, elaborate design. Yes, its nice and, yes, it is definitely original, but how does it look at 1 1/2"? How does it transfer in black and white? Can it be embroidered as easily as it can be printed?

These are all questions that have to be asked in the design process. Always remember the K.I.S.S model (Keep It Simple Sweetheart). This is a golden rule. It doesn't matter if it is embroidered or printed; every color has a price tag attached to it. Cost of production is always a factor when producing quality promotional pieces. You also have to factor in that if the logo is small enough, will it effectively go through the four color printing process? If your logo has 9 colors and it is printed at 1 1/2" tall, you may get a blob of colors that are unrecognizable.

Tag It and Bag It

A tag line is a great way to be remembered. If, for example, your marketing includes a radio spot, the listeners can't see a logo, but a great tag line can be an instant auditory visual. It doesn't have to be a tag line either. A catchy jingle is nothing more than an elongated tag line. "Give me a break...give me a break...Break me off a piece..." Don't tell me that you didn't finish singing that.

Commit to It

Once you have a logo, commit to it. Incorporate the colors into your web page, your letterhead, even the color scheme of your showroom if you have a brick & mortar place of business. Once you have it all worked out, own it because if you don't, it will promote you as being wishy-washy and can go as far as to concern people of your reliability if your logo changes at the drop of a hat.

Now once you have your logo in place, you can modify it

as long as the core concept is there. The Niki icon has changed since it was first created, but it is still the swoosh that people the world over have come to associate with the name.

Final Thoughts

I want to personally thank you for taking the time to read this book and I hope that it has truly helped you to go out and create the life you deserve. A life with a business that you work on and not in; one that allows you the freedom to spend more of your valuable time with friends and family doing what you want and not what you have to in order to make ends meet.

Thanks for reading take care.

www.ingramcontent.com/pod-product-compliance
Lightning Source LLC
Chambersburg PA
CBHW040928180526
45159CB00002BA/662